2/97

KOMODO DRAGONS

KOMODO DRAGONS

THANE MAYNARD

THE CHILD'S WORLD®, INC.

Photo Credits
Comstock: cover, 2, 6, 10, 16, 23, 24, 30
Edward Maruska/Cincinnati Zoo: 9, 13, 15, 19, 20
S. David Jenike: 26, 29

Printed in the United States of America.

Library of Congress Cataloging-in-Publication Data
Maynard, Thane.
Komodo dragons/Thane Maynard.
p.   cm.
Includes index.
Summary: Describes the physical characteristics, habitat,
and life cycle of this species of giant lizard, which is
found only in Indonesia.
ISBN 1-56766-266-8
1. Komodo dragon--Juvenile literature.   [1. Komodo
dragon.   2. Lizards.]
I. Title.
QL666.L29M39   1996
597.95--dc20   95-26392
  [B]   CIP
                              AC

TABLE OF CONTENTS

Some people think that dragons are only make-believe animals—like the flying, fire-breathing dragons in books and movies. But if you travel to the far-off islands of a country called Indonesia, you can find real-life dragons! Komodo dragons.

Komodo dragons don't fly. They don't breathe fire, either. So why are they called "dragons"? Because they are the biggest **lizards** in the world. They look like little dragons.

Komodo dragons are the biggest lizards in the world.

WHERE DO KOMODO DRAGONS LIVE?

Komodo dragons are a type of lizard called a *monitor*. They come from the Komodo Island area of Indonesia, near the northwest shore of Australia. It is one of the harshest and hottest places in the world. Often, the temperature is over 100° F. Sometimes it even gets as hot as 110° F.

On the hottest days, dragons escape the heat by getting out of the sun. They rest in underground burrows. But in the morning, when they first wake up, they lie in the sun to warm up. They do that on cooler days, too. That is because, like all lizards, they are **reptiles**. Reptiles are **cold-blooded** animals. They need outside heat (like sunlight) to warm them up.

Komodo dragons need to warm their bodies.

Like most lizards, Komodo dragons are active during the day and sleep at night. Both males and females dig burrows. They sleep in their burrows at night and often rest in them during the hot day. They like to dig their dens in open hillsides or alongside streams.

Komodo dragons are active during the day.

WHAT DO KOMODO DRAGONS LOOK LIKE?

Reptiles have scales instead of soft skin. Komodo dragons are covered with rough scales. These scales are bumpy and look like armor. The bumps help protect the lizards as they move around.

The dark color of adult dragons helps them soak up the heat of the sun.

Komodo dragons have bumpy scales.

Komodo dragons walk on bowed legs. Their tails swish back and forth to help them balance. They hold their heads high so that they can see and smell the slightest hint of a nearby animal.

Komodo dragons hold their heads high to smell.

Adult dragons can grow to be over 10 feet long. They can weigh as much as 250 pounds! Males are usually bigger than females.

Komodo dragons are very strong. They also have claws that are two to three inches long. These claws help the dragons to dig holes and to grasp their prey.

Komodo dragons have long claws.

WHAT DO KOMODO DRAGONS EAT?

Komodo dragons hunt and eat other animals. Animals that eat other animals are called **predators**. Komodo dragons are fierce hunters. They eat anything they can catch, from rats to goats. They can catch and eat animals that are much bigger than they are. Sometimes they even eat water buffalo, which can weigh over 1,000 pounds!

Komodo dragons are fierce hunters.

These giant lizards don't have very big teeth—but they have a lot of them! These teeth are very sharp, just perfect for biting chunks of meat. The edges of the teeth have ridges. The ridges are good for biting and holding onto their dinner.

Komodo dragon teeth are good for biting and holding onto prey.

21

Komodo dragons stick their tongues out all the time. They don't do it to tease each other. They do it for the same reason snakes do—to smell! They pick up smells as they wave their tongues through the air. That's why the tongue is forked, or shaped like a Y. That gives the tongue a wider surface to tell which direction a smell is coming from.

A Komodo dragon uses its tongue to smell.

Usually Komodo dragons wait quietly for their dinner to come to them. If they need to, though, they can run as fast as 8 miles per hour! They can't run that fast for very long, but it can help them catch their dinner.

Komodo dragons wait patiently for their dinner.

HOW ARE BABY KOMODO DRAGONS BORN?

Like most reptiles, Komodo dragons hatch from eggs. Dragon mothers lay their eggs on the ground. Then they dig a big hole and bury the eggs under the sand. This keeps the eggs nice and warm—about 81° F. It also protects them until they hatch. Hatching takes about eight months. Mother dragons usually lay between 10 and 27 eggs.

Dragon eggs have a soft, smooth shell. They are much bigger than chicken eggs. In fact, they are usually bigger than a baseball! That's a good thing, because baby dragons are about 16 inches long when they hatch.

A mother dragon lays her eggs on the ground.

HOW DO BABY KOMODO DRAGONS GROW UP?

Baby dragons take care of themselves right from the beginning. When they are very young, they eat insects and small rodents. Soon, though, they move on to bigger animals. Komodo dragons grow up fast. In their first six months they grow to nearly three feet long—twice as big as when they hatch.

Baby Komodo dragons have many more spots than their parents do. That helps them hide from other hungry animals. They are also good climbers when they are young, and often live up in trees. That is probably to help them keep away from adult dragons. The adults will eat them if they get the chance!

Baby Komodo dragons have more spots then the adult dragons.

ARE KOMODO DRAGONS IN DANGER?

Komodo dragons are rare animals. They live on only a few islands. As more and more people move into those areas, there is less and less room for the dragons.

For the dragons to survive, they need protected areas where they are free to roam and hunt, as they have for millions of years. Long live the dragons!

Komodo dragons are rare animals.

GLOSSARY

cold-blooded (kold-BLUDD-ded)
Needing outside heat to stay warm. Komodo dragons warm their bodies by lying in the the sun.

lizard (LIZZ-urd)
A reptile that has a long body, legs, and a tapering tail. Komodo dragons are lizards. Dinosaurs were lizards, too.

predator (PRED-uh-tur)
An animal that hunts and kills other animals for food. Komodo dragons eat any animal they can catch.

reptile (REPP-tyle)
An animal that is cold-blooded and has a skin covered with scales. Lizards, snakes, and turtles are all reptiles.

INDEX